Boscastle   25 Jun 85

Elizabeth Palmer   Palmer

D1799584

NORTH CORNWALL
in the OLD DAYS

Joan Rendell

Bossiney Books

First published in 1983
by Bossiney Books
St Teath, Bodmin, Cornwall.
Designed, printed and bound in Great Britain by
A. Wheaton & Co., Ltd, Exeter.

All rights reserved

© Joan Rendell 1983

ISBN 0 906456 79 7

ACKNOWLEDGMENTS

Cover photograph by courtesy of the Royal Institution of Cornwall coloured by Paul Honeywill.

The picture postcards used in this book have been kindly provided by Peter Dryden, Jim Ferrett and the author, and other old views of North Cornwall by the Royal Institution of Cornwall and Launceston Museum.

ABOUT THE AUTHOR –
AND THE BOOK

Joan Rendell is one of Bossiney's most prolific authors. This is her sixth title for the Cornish cottage publishers, and she has contributed to the widely acclaimed *The Cornish Year Book*.

She made her debut for Bossiney in 1979 with *Along the Bude Canal*, following it with such diverse titles as *Hawker Country*, *Lundy*, *Gateway to Cornwall* and *Cornish Churches*.

The daughter of a St Austell father and a Helston mother, Joan Rendell has travelled extensively: to every country in Europe – except Iceland – to the Middle East, North Africa and the Americas. She is a frequent lecturer and contributes to a variety of publications, including *This England* and *Cornish Life*. Her authorship encompasses such contrasting works as books on Matchbox Labels and Country Crafts, Flower Arrangements and Corn Dollies. Her passion for matchbox labels began at the age of eight, and her collection, now totalling 205,000, is one of the largest in the world.

In September 1980 Joan Rendell was initiated as a Bard of the Cornish Gorseth, taking the name of *Scryfer Weryn* – Writer of Werrington. She lives in the Parish of Werrington, through which the Bude Canal once flowed.

In 1958 she was awarded the MBE and in 1977 the Queen's Silver Jubilee Medal.

North Cornwall in the Old Days is a new venture for Joan Rendell, providing the text for a fine harvest of old photographs and picture postcards.

Counting North Cornwall as an area roughly stretching from Newquay to the Cornwall–Devon border, and coming inland to the extent of Launceston and Bodmin, it covers such fascinating Cornish territory as Bude and Boscastle, Tintagel and Wadebridge, St Columb and Padstow – and much more.

'At one time,' writes the author, 'North Cornwall was known as the forgotten land, probably at a time when many of the photographs in this book were taken.'

'North Cornwall will no longer be the forgotten land after this title,' says publisher Michael Williams. 'We have searched diligently for old photographs and are deeply indebted to individuals and organisations who have co-operated so splendidly. These pictures and Joan's perceptive text combine to give us many facets of a nostalgic way of North Cornish life, turning the calendars back as if we are on some magical time-machine.'

The Author in the robes of a Bard of the Cornish Gorseth.

NORTH CORNWALL IN THE OLD DAYS

At one time North Cornwall was known as the forgotten land, probably at the time when many of the photographs in this book were taken.

However, not any more – today North Cornwall is a thriving tourist area as well as being a rich agricultural district. The beauty of its scenery has in no way changed.

Its villages may have got bigger, its farms more mechanised and its residents more sophisticated, but its natural wonders and magnificence remain as they always were, for man cannot pit his frail strength against the towering cliffs, the crashing waves and some of the areas of wild land which still remain.

North Cornwall cannot boast of a settled climate and over the years correspondents writing to friends and relatives back home have made some succinct comments on the picture postcards which have been a part of the holiday ritual for so long now.

On some of the cards illustrated in this book the senders have written variously of the weather as being 'very windy', 'too hot', 'very cold and snowing here' (that at Delabole at the turn of the century), 'having lovely weather', 'weather very disappointing', 'weather glorious', 'rather dull', 'gales have been the order of the day' (at Bude), 'rough weather on Saturday' (at Wadebridge in August), 'having grand weather' (at Newquay in July 1907) and 'very wet and stormy today' (at Newquay in July 1908). Surely something to suit all tastes there and a

Right: The sailing coaster *Lively* of Bideford at Boscastle quay in 1905.

vivid reminder that North Cornwall can produce all sorts of surprises, even in the height of the summer!

The zenith of the picture postcard sending era was probably during the years from the turn of the century until the outbreak of World War I. 'Buying your cards' was one of the first duties of any self-respecting holidaymaker but the selection offered was not always to the taste of the customer: 'No decent views of this place' wrote a correspondent contemptuously on a postcard of Trelights village sent in 1905 to someone at St Teath.

Several correspondents referred on postcards shown in this book to the fact that the items were sent for a collection. The greatest thrill was being able to buy a card which showed someone you actually knew being 'snapped' or posing as part of the scene. A postcard of Port Gaverne sent in 1907 from 'Kate' to 'Jessie' in faraway London had the excited message on the back, 'This is Aunt Maria and the two children', the trio shown posing rather selfconsciously by the seawall, obviously having just happened to be coming along the road when the photographer was at work.

Of course, not everyone appreciated the peace and beauty of North Cornwall. 'Shall be glad to get back to Bournemouth', wrote M.W. from Bude in 1912 and 'Thank goodness this is my last week in Cornwall' a Mr George penned rather sourly to Mrs George in Deal, Kent. Others were more romantic – 'This place would be all right for a honeymoon, so quiet and out of the way' was the message on the back of a view of Marhamchurch sent in June 1909.

North Cornwall has so much to offer – bustling seaside resorts, wild moorland, awe–inspiring cliffs, great sandy beaches, hidden coves, flower-filled country lanes, secluded villages. The old legends still live; Celtic saints, who often arrived in Cornwall in miraculous ways, have left their imprint, especially in village names.

Some of the magic of North Cornwall has been captured by the camera. Timeless, ageless, the northern part of our glorious county will forever weave its spell on all who live in it or visit it. Perhaps the photographs in this book will help to convey that spell.

Right: Teresa Mallett photographed at Port Gaverne in 1906 by Herbert Hughes. Some of the vintage Cornish photographs were the work of Hughes, a mining engineer in the collieries. He and photographer friends visited Cornwall for several years in succession between the late 1890s and just before the 1914–18 War. Some of their memorable photographs of that period appear inside these pages. Like the great Newlyn painter, Stanhope Forbes, Hughes had supreme talent for using local people as his models. Teresa may no longer be at Port Gaverne but it is of course possible that children or relations of hers still remain in this North Cornish village.

Towan Beach remains one of Newquay's most popular
bathing beaches, just as it was when this picture was
taken at the turn of the century, but all the bathing
machines disappeared long ago.

Newquay, the largest town in North Cornwall, sprawls
over a vast area and in summertime is packed with
visitors. At one time a small port, it is now geared almost
entirely to the tourist industry.

Newquay, reflected the Poet Laureate, 'is what all the
coast of Cornwall would have been like if the speculative
builders had had their way ... It has vitality and
vulgarity.' The beaches hereabouts are not only beautiful,
they have evocative names: Fistral and Lusty Glaze,
Towan and Tolcarne are only some of them. The town
grew up on the north bank of the Gannel, a river and
estuary, where ships were built in the days when
Newquay was a commercial port.

Another photographic gem by Herbert Hughes taken on
25 June 1910 at Newquay.

Peter Dryden, who hails from Falmouth, is a dedicated collector of old Cornish picture postcards, many of which appear here. About this card, he says: 'The group of buildings centre left were called Speculation Cellars and the Cosy Nook Theatre used to be a tent erected on the left in the foreground. It rattled so much that sometimes the Concert Party could not be heard.'

Nothing depicts the transformation of Newquay more vividly than these two old postcards of Newquay harbour on the right. Together they reveal the various faces of Newquay: the fishing boats and sailing coasters, the railway, the paddle steamer in the bay and the hotels on the clifftop. When these cards were printed the railway was beginning to change the tourist character of Cornwall but this line was essentially for commerce.

The upper card reads: 'We are having a nice time at Newquay today. We have been to Polzeath, Harlyn, Lanow, Amble and Trevanger. Hope father is keeping well. Return on Monday. Love Ellen.' Intriguingly this card posted in Newquay with a 1d stamp showing the head of King George V was addressed to No. 2 Coronation Terrace, Bodmin!

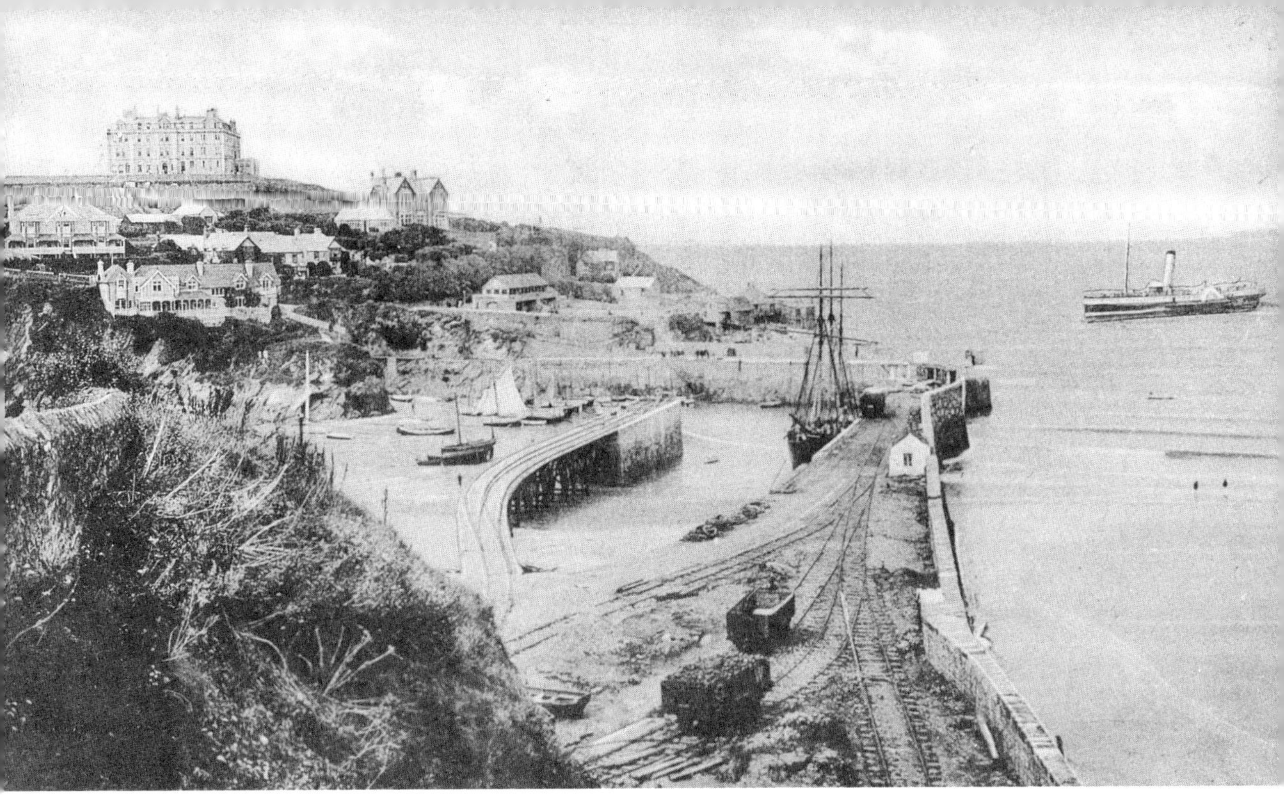

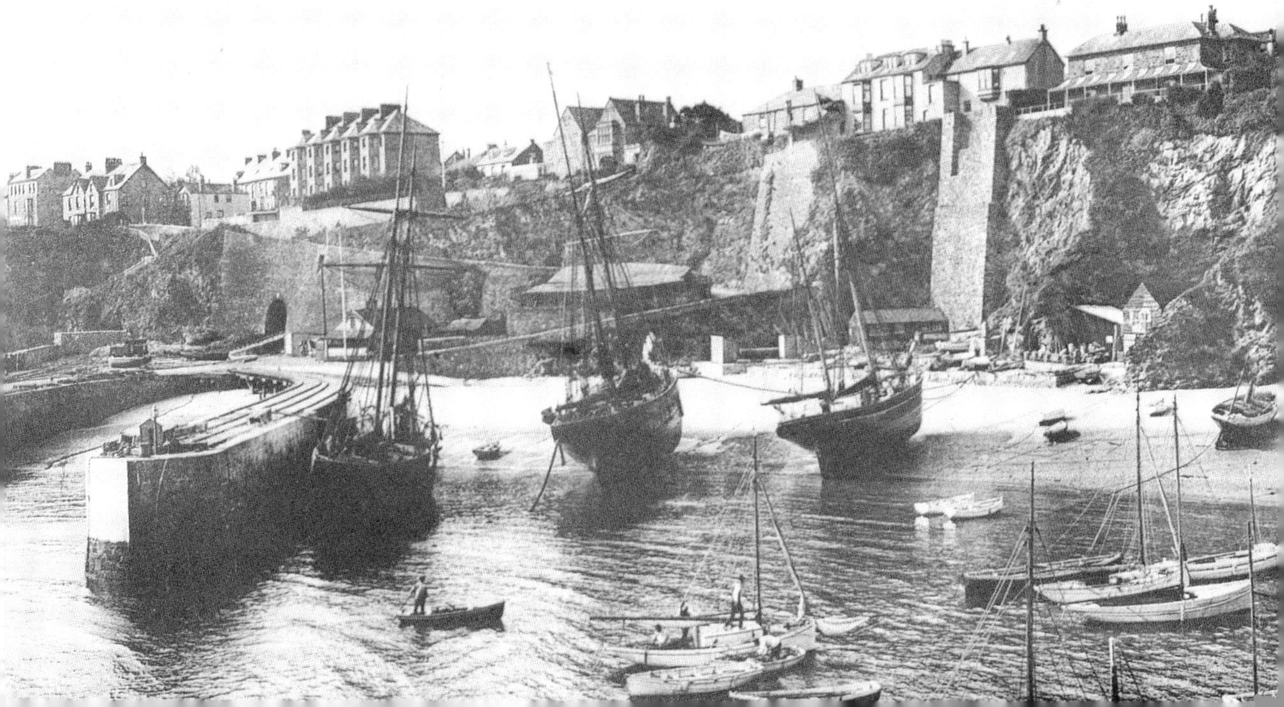

Two views of Bank Street, Newquay. Many of Newquay's shops now cater for the holidaymaker and the time has gone when the family grocer occupied a corner site and delivered customers' orders over a wide area.

Launching the Newquay Lifeboat. Newquay lifeboat station was opened in 1861 and the first boat, given by an anonymous lady, was called *Joshua*. Unfortunately it only carried out one rescue before being taken out of service because it was riddled with dry rot. It was replaced in 1865 with another boat of the same name. Until 1895 Newquay lifeboat was kept in a boathouse in Fore Street, but in that year a special house was built for it near the end of the headland which protects the harbour and from there it could easily be launched into deep water. The town's first lifeboat cost just £157.

The Huer's Hut in Newquay in 1914. These little huts
were the vantage point for the huer, the man who kept
watch from the cliffs for the pilchard shoals to arrive. The
watch-houses were strongly built because sometimes the
huer had to remain in them several days before spotting a
shoal. When he caught sight of the turbulence in the
water which signified the approach of the shoal he would
shout through a huge megaphone-like instrument
'Hevva, hevva' meaning 'a shoal' in Cornish. This would
be the signal for the fishing boats to put to sea and they
were guided by the huer, who waved white banners to
show them the location of the fish. As soon as the boats
were in the appropriate position, he would yell, 'Shoot
the seine'. Onshore everyone would be waiting with great
excitement for the catch to be brought ashore. The huer's
hut at Newquay is still maintained in a good state of
preservation.

Tucking pilchards at the beginning of the century.

A seine was the forerunner of today's fishermen's co-operative. It was usually composed of three boats, each seine having its own stretch of sea in which to operate. The seine boat was rowed by six men and carried the huge net, often a quarter of a mile in length and weighing several tons. The boat encircled a shoal of fish – usually pilchards – the net 'scooping' them up. It was then pulled inshore by capstans erected on the beach. A tuck net was used to bring the fish into the boats.

Beach Road, Newquay: Fashions for both ladies and gentlemen have greatly changed since this picture was taken. The visitors who walk up and down the roads in Newquay today are far more scantily clad than the Edwardian holidaymakers shown on this card. On the right are some old fish cellars.

Porth, near Newquay. On the northern arm of the bay is
Trevelgue Head where there are the remains of an Iron
Age cliff castle.

Left: Lawry's Mill near Newquay. Water mills were a
familiar sight in North Cornwall, mostly for grinding
corn.

Above: Crantock is a village popular with tourists now.
The church has Norman stones in its walls and the tower
dates from the thirteenth and fifteenth centuries.

Below: A picnic on Holywell Beach, south of Newquay.

Above: Newlyn East. This quaint little building attached to the side of a sturdy stone house was probably a tollhouse in the days of the turnpike roads. In the church with its fine medieval tower lie many members of the Arundell family.

Below: Mawgan-in-Pydar also knew the Arundell family. Their Elizabethan mansion called Lanherne is now a convent. The village still retains much of its old-world charm although there has been a lot of new building and an RAF station is situated not far away.

St Columb Minor Church.

Right: Trerice, in the parish of Newlyn East, three miles from Newquay, is a former home of the famous Arundell family. Built in the sixteenth-century it is now owned by the National Trust and is open to the public. The imposing grey stone house is tucked away in a delightful valley and has been little altered in its long life. The window of the Great Hall, seen on the left in the upper postcard, has twenty-four lights and no less than 576 panes of glass, much of it original sixteenth-century. The north wing, shown on this card as almost a ruin with windows bricked up, has been restored. It was dismantled in the 1860s after a severe gale when it was considered to be in a dangerous condition. According to the caption on the lower card this is an 'oriel window'. This fine two-storied bay window lights the Solar on the first floor of Trerice and is sixteenth-century. The Solar is now called the drawingroom and was probably always the principal sitting room of the house.

A delightfully rural scene from the days when horses and carts were the main form of transport in North Cornwall and Town Mills and Bridge Hill at St Columb were usually very busy.

St Columb Major's streets remain narrow today and, although not easy for present-day traffic, the town has retained much of its original character. Through the streets of St Columb the annual hurling matches take place on Shrove Tuesday and the second Saturday in Lent, when representatives of Town and Country battle for possession of the silver ball.

One of Cornwall's folklore figures in the sport of Cornish wrestling was James Polkinghorne who was innkeeper at the Red Lion. Polkinghorne, in his prime, was champion wrestler and a tablet on the wall of the Red Lion commemorates his great match with Abraham Cann, the champion of Devon, which took place before 17,000 spectators in 1826.

Herbert Hughes and his colleagues may not have realised it but they were pioneer photographers of the great Cornish seascapes. Here they are at work above Watergate Bay. The road that snakes up the hill beyond the hotel in the direction of Padstow would have been used by relatively few cars in 1909 and no doubt if Mr Hughes and his colleagues came back today, they would see many changes – for the worse – in North Cornwall, but this narrow twisting coastal road linking Newquay and Padstow remains one of the great Cornish experiences.

The North Cornwall coastal scenery is magnificent and Porthcothan is one of the unspoilt coves which abound along this coast. At one time Porthcothan was popular with smugglers and a mile or so inland there are still traces in the valley of the thousand yard long cave where the smugglers hid kegs of brandy and other goods brought in by their luggers.

The celebrated author, D.H. Lawrence, lived at Porthcothan for a while. He may have liked the place but he did not like the people: 'They have got the souls of insects … they are all afraid – that's why they are so mean. I have never in my life come across such innerly selfish people.' It is interesting to speculate what events may have triggered this incredible assessment of the locals. Later, when in West Cornwall, Lawrence and his wife again were at odds with a Cornish community and were accused, by some, of being spies in the 1914–18 War.

A tea garden at Harlyn Bay offered refreshment in a pleasantly tree-shaded corner. It was in the early years of this century that the Reverend William Iago and the Reverend Sabine Baring-Gould of *Onward Christian Soldiers* fame, took part in the excavation of an Iron Age cemetery (*below*) at Harlyn Bay under the direction of Mr Reddie Mallet. This was rated one of the most dramatic archaeological finds of the twentieth century – it revealed 130 graves, numerous skeletons and some rare pieces of metalwork.

Padstow in its time was the haunt of the legendary
Westcountry seadogs. Sir John Hawkins, Sir Martin
Frobisher and Sir Walter Raleigh all came here. Padstow
history has always had a seafaring tradition: trading or
fishing or shipbuilding. The whole of medieval Padstow –
including the harbour – belonged to the Priory at Bodmin
and harbour tithes were paid to the Abbot.

A great hazard to shipping which limited the growth of
the harbour was the Doom Bar, a sand bar at the mouth of
the Camel Estuary. Cornish fishermen have long been a
superstitious race. A *West Briton* report, published in
1848, said: 'Within the last few weeks, the fishing boats of
Padstow have caught several thousands of herrings, but
one boat being more unfortunate than the others, some
persons persuaded the crew that the boat was bewitched.
They then determined to break the charm by nailing a
horseshoe to the bottom of the boat, which they did, and
the next night caught 1,400 fish, which confirmed the
belief that the boat had been bewitched!'

On May Day the streets of Padstow ring to the sound of music and song when the 'Obby 'Oss celebrations take place. The 'Osses and their processions wind around the narrow streets of the town and around the harbour area. This ancient ceremony has survived to the present day and is now a great attraction and an occasion for a 'day out' for people from all over the county. Originally this was a fertility rite and welcomed also the coming of summer and the sun which would ripen the crops. The 'Oss is a very strenuous undertaking for the man who has to prance the streets all day, encouraged by a 'teaser'. Streets and buildings were always decorated with leafy branches in full spring greenery and the celebrations included – as today – the consuming of intoxicating liquor to keep one going.

Padstow Harbour and the Camel Estuary.

'Obby 'Oss group at Padstow earlier this century.

Prideaux Place, Padstow, in 1906. This is the old home of the Prideaux family, standing on the hill just above the church. It is said to have been built on a site of a monastery which was destroyed by the Danes. The stately Elizabethan house is reached through a majestic gateway which stands by the road and it contains some notable art treasures, as well as Grinling Gibbons carving and a fireplace and staircase from Stowe, former home of the Grenvilles near Kilkhampton, now totally destroyed.

A Garden Party at Prideaux Place thought to be about
1899. The house is still the home of the Prideaux-Brune
family.

Right: Little Petherick lies in a valley, the stream being a tributary of the River Camel. The church was much renovated in the nineteenth century but still has some old bench ends. One of its features is the Molesworth Chapel.

Above: Here's another fine example of Herbert Hughes'
photography: Harbour Cove in 1907 with Padstow
lifeboat and a Padstow-registered steamer anchored off.
Since Hughes' day the lifeboat has moved around the
coast to the deeper water off Trevose.

Left: The location of this old photograph is undoubtedly
Market Square, Padstow, but the date is uncertain – some
believe possibly during the 1914–18 War. In that event
perhaps some of these Padstow children are still living in
the area.

St Minver lies across the Camel Estuary from Padstow and is a large parish with three churches: St Minver, St Enodoc and St Michael. There is a North Cornwall tradition that the boy Jesus came ashore at St Minver to get fresh water for the ship on which he sailed with Joseph of Arimathea – a tin-buying excursion – and Jesus Well, standing in a field, still provides a water supply today. In the olden days children suffering from whooping cough were brought here to drink the waters. St Minefreda's Church (*above*) standing on the side of the valley, is a landmark visible for many miles across the North Cornwall landscape. It has a fine steeple, a not too common sight hereabouts.

St Enodoc and St Enoder are often confused. St Enodoc Church (*below right*) stands close to the sea and is almost hidden among sand dunes. For many years it was buried in the sand and then in the 1800s it was uncovered and its slightly crooked little spire points it out to the visitor who will find it well worth a visit. The one bell in the tower of the church was recovered from a ship wrecked off the coast nearby.

St Michael's Church at Porthilly, Rock, in St Minver
parish, was also buried in the sand at one time. The
present building is on the site of a very ancient chapel
here on the banks of the River Camel.

Stoptide is now a popular residential area of Rock and commands beautiful views of the Camel Estuary.

Rock village (*left*) now straggles for a long distance up the road from the water. It is a popular spot with sailing enthusiasts and has also developed very much as a residential area over the past decade. When this photograph was taken it consisted of little more than the buildings shown in the picture. The photograph (*below*) was taken in 1906. The old warehouse on the quay has now been converted into the clubhouse for the Rock Sailing Club.

Tredrizzick, St Minver. Many Cornish villages cluster around the Methodist Chapel, which was usually built as close as possible to the local community.

Doyden Castle stands out conspicuously on the cliffs at Port Quin. It is a strange Gothic folly and has been used as a TV setting, first in Winston Graham's *Poldark* and, more recently, in Daphne du Maurier's *Jamaica Inn*.

Wadebridge, situated at the head of the twisting Camel
Estuary, is roughly eight miles from the sea. The name
Wadebridge is thought to have been derived from the
Latin, *Vadum*, meaning ford. In modern times the bridge
at Wadebridge is the scene of long traffic hold-ups in the
holiday season but in the days when the railway was
operating most of the traffic came by rail.

The Bodmin–Wadebridge line was the first railway in
Cornwall – 1830 – and the second in all England. The
Great Western, by stretching itself into Cornwall, first
thought in terms of goods traffic – items like tin and china
clay and fish – but it was soon helping to sow the seeds of
Cornish tourism and slowly but surely began to change
the character of North Cornwall.

The Bridge on Wool, Wadebridge, showing the angles in
the wall where pedestrians can avoid the traffic. The
bridge has been much widened over the years since this
picture was taken.

Wadebridge showing the bridge
and the estuary and the railway station.

Wadebridge's fine bridge is known as the Bridge on Wool because it was given to the town by one Thomas Lovibond, who had made his money in the wool trade. An old legend has it that bales of wool actually formed the foundations of the bridge but that has been disproved. For centuries the bridge has been known as the longest and fairest bridge in Cornwall. Its thirteen arches span 320 feet across the River Camel.

The steamship *Dunraven* and other coastal sailing vessels moored below the bridge at Wadebridge. Even in this century sailing ships came up to Wadebridge at high tide to load and unload at the wharves below the bridge. They are still in use today.

This part of Molesworth Street, Wadebridge, has not altered a great deal in appearance since this picture was taken but the slow pace of life depicted here has long since disappeared. The Molesworths were the principal landowners in the district and Pencarrow, the Molesworth family home off the Bodmin road, is open to the public in the summer.

St Petroc's Church, Bodmin, is the largest parish church in the whole county. St Petroc was to Cornwall what St Patrick was to Ireland. Scattered over Devon and Cornwall are churches dedicated to him. He founded the monastery at Padstow and the Priory here in Bodmin in the sixth century.

Mount Folly Square, Bodmin, the Assize Court with its
three open arches on the right.

Bodmin, in the old days, would have made an ideal touring centre, being roughly
twelve miles from the north and south coasts, and on the south-western edge of
Bodmin Moor. Moreover it made a good base for anglers using the River Camel.

The county town has had a colourful history. One grisly episode related to the
suppression of Arundell's Rebellion in the year 1549. Sir Anthony Kingston, the
Provost-Marshal, wrote to the Mayor of Bodmin, one Nicholas Boyer, announcing
that he wished to dine with the Mayor. Arrangements were made and before
dinner the Provost told the Mayor that gallows must be erected that evening as an
execution must be performed before the day ended. The Mayor complied and,
when dinner was over, the Provost was taken to the gallows.

'Are they strong enough?' asked the wily Sir Anthony as the two men stood
before them.

'Yes,' replied the unsuspecting Mayor.

'Well, then,' said the Provost, 'get up speedily, for they have been prepared for
you, for you have been a busy rebel!'

The town clock was usually the centrepiece of most market towns and Bodmin was no exception. It still keeps accurate time and is a boon to townsfolk and travellers alike.

Below: Bodmin's Fore Street has changed little in appearance from when this photograph was taken, except that many shop fronts have been modernised, and the Royal Hotel, with its glass canopy over the main entrance, has long gone.

Right: The market house in Bodmin, with its iron gates and mouldings of bullocks' heads, is no longer used for its original purpose. After closing as a market it housed a laundry for many years and now shops. The little seventeenth-century Guildhall is hidden between the shops on the right hand side of the photograph.

Looking down Fore Street.

Fore Street with the market house on the left.

Inland Cornwall is often underestimated and St Kew is a
good example. This lovely parish is punctuated with hills
and valleys, narrow lanes and little-known hamlets. It is
an area rich in Iron Age hillforts some even linked with
the Arthurian legends.

The Cornish Arms at Pendoggett, a hamlet between Delabole and St Endellion. Now modernised, the Cornish Arms is unquestionably one of the finest inns in the Westcountry with an outstanding reputation for good food.

Left: St Teath is a busy village sandwiched between two main roads. In 1914 the writer of this card said on it that in the morning she attended a service at the chapel shown in the photograph.

A celebrated seventeenth-century resident was Anne Jeffries who acquired a national fame or notoriety as a healer. Sick people travelled hundreds of miles to St Teath to meet her. This parish is a haunted corner of North Cornwall for when the wind is in a certain direction the old folk said they could hear the cries of Squire Cheney's ghost hounds out hunting.

Port Isaac was once a busy fishing port with boatbuilding
yards. It was also a popular haunt for smugglers, its
architectural jig-saw puzzle proving a real headache for
the preventive men. The closeness of the cottages enabled
families to tap warnings to one another on the walls of the
neighbouring buildings. In the days of these photographs
Port Isaac Road Station, roughly three miles away, was on
the main Waterloo to Padstow line.

Unloading a coaster by pony and cart at Port Isaac.

Right: Even in the days when this picture was taken that
famous Westcountry newspaper *The Western Morning
News* was popular reading!

The main street of Port Isaac earlier this century. Today it is a trap for unwary motorists. Despite the march of progress and the growth of tourism, Port Isaac still manages to generate an old world charm – due largely to its nooks and crannies – while the view up the coast to Tintagel must surely rank as one of the finest in the Westcountry.

Such a grand sounding name for a tiny but picturesque
corner of old Port Isaac. It is also known as Squeezibelly
Alley, which in some places is no more than eighteen
inches wide. It leads from the main street through the
middle of someone's house.

Port Gaverne, still a sheltered cove, was once busy with shipping slate from the famous Delabole Quarry, some six miles away, to all parts of the British Isles. Before the coming of the railway as many as thirty wagons and one hundred horses were employed to load a sixty ton vessel here (*below right*). In those times, the sea was the highway for south-western commerce. Boats often brought back coal from South Wales.

The postcard of Port Gaverne above shows the correspondent's relatives – 'Aunt Maria and the two children'.

The coast at Port Gaverne.

Delabole Slate Quarry: Slate has been quarried here for
hundreds of years and these are two of the earliest
photographs, taken in 1886. In the quarry's earlier days it
tended to expand outwards rather than downwards and
some homes were engulfed, just as motorway building
'swallows' homes today. For many years one cottage
remained with quarry workings all round it, but it has
long since disappeared as the quarry became larger and
larger over the years.

Today Delabole Quarry is so deep that standing on its edge and looking down into the far distant depths one sees huge yellow dumper trucks and other gigantic machines looking just like Dinky toys, they are so far away 'down the hole'. It is in fact the deepest man-made hole in Europe, being more than 500 feet deep and more than a mile in circumference.

Slate has been the life-blood of Delabole for generations.
Slates from the quarries have been used in buildings all
over the country and slate splitting by hand is a highly
skilled craft. The quarry has greatly increased in size since
this picture was taken.

Right: Lower Pengelly, Delabole, looked a pretty desolate
place when this photograph was taken. Note the
slate-hung houses making good use of the local product.
This is a rare view of the quarry entrance in Edwardian
times. It is now much changed and improved and the
quarry complex includes a museum, craft and gift shop
and demonstrations of the ancient craft of slate splitting.

Delabole High Street as this postcard is captioned looks like a dirt road when this picture was taken. No-one would dare to walk in the road pushing a pram these days! Delabole is a long, straggling village and 'High Street' is part of the main road which links Bude with the popular resorts on the edge of the Camel Estuary – places like Polzeath, Daymer Bay and Rock.

Camelford, Fore Street

Above: Camelford Town Hall has a unique weathervane – a golden camel crowns the cupola. The appearance of the main street, which is now part of the busy A39 road, has changed little in appearance from when this picture was taken but the cobbles have disappeared and the road surface is much different!

Right: Camelford's Darlington Hotel is still a popular hostelry. The Camelford area has strong links with the legend of King Arthur. Bodmin Moor rises behind it with Brown Willy, the highest point in Cornwall, not far away.

Camelford, on the strength of its name, must come into
any Arthurian assessment of Cornwall. On the surface
there is no obvious Court of Camelot quality, but being so
near Slaughter Bridge – where some say Arthur fought his
last battle – and only five miles from Tintagel, Camelford
on the River Camel has long been a favourite in the search
for Camelot. Some even say Arthur's grave is on the banks
of the Camel. Arthur has always been a magical figure and
Tennyson did much to project his image beyond the
bounds of mere imagination. The sites claimed for his
grave are manifold, yet it is always to the Cornish legends
that one usually turns first; his name is revered to this day
in the county and immortalised in the motto of the Old
Cornwall Societies.

Trebarwith – the road to the sea. The great Gull Rock
stands off Trebarwith Strand, which is open to the full
force of the Atlantic. Trebarwith personifies some of the
best of our North Cornish coast, cliffs and caves, sand and
sea and sky. On a diamond-sharp day you can understand
why a celebrated painter like Thomas Creswick chose to
paint many pictures here. At high water the beach is
totally covered, but the sea smashing over the dark rocks
and racing up the causeway can be a thrilling spectacle.
This is a dangerous coastline.

An attractively coloured slate is quarried around here and
is much in demand for fireplaces, garden walls and other
decorative uses. In the days when the local quarries along
the cliffs were operating, men worked with the tides
around the clock. When the tide was in they blasted;
when the tide was out they went down and collected the
slate, either by ladders or in buckets operated by a winch.

Above: Treligga could be termed a typical North Cornish hamlet. Not nearly as remote as it used to be when this picture was taken, but still a quiet haven of peace for those escaping from the hustle and bustle of modern life.

Trenale is now almost a part of Tintagel.

One of the most photographed buildings in the whole of
Cornwall. The Old Post Office at Tintagel is a
fourteenth-century building built to the plan of a
medieval manor house, with a large hall. In the
nineteenth century it was used for nearly fifty years as a
letter receiving office for the district, hence its name. It is
now owned by the National Trust and is open to the
public. The Trust has restored it and, standing as it does
in the main street of Tintagel, it is visited by thousands of
people every year. Long before it was taken over by the
National Trust, it was allowed to get into a state of some
decay in the early twentieth century. The writer of the
card (*above right*) recorded that when she visited the Old
Post Office in 1908 it was still inhabited although no
longer a Post Office.

What is known as King Arthur's Castle at Tintagel is the
ruins of a Plantagenet fortress and nearby have been
discovered remains of a Celtic monastery and a Norman
chapel. Despite the missing masonry of the Castle, it
remains an awe-inspiring sight. This great headland
towers 270 feet above the sea and covers 27 acres.

The River Valency winds its way right through the lower part of Boscastle towards the sea, helping to form the harbour.

Boscastle is one of the most attractive and picturesque of all the North Cornish villages and is extremely popular with visitors. The pretty white-walled cottages are still here.

This surprising view of Boscastle, taken in Edwardian times, makes it look almost like a modern inland town of quite large proportions.

Twisting roads with hairpin bends (*right*) lead down to the harbour at Boscastle, a shelter for which many ships have run in their time. Nearby is the blowhole in the cliffs, which one novelist christened the Devil's bellows. The harbour entrance (*below*) is difficult to see from seawards as the river angles its way through the cleft in the cliffs, and so the harbour is spared the full force of the Atlantic rollers. Profile Rock on the right uncannily resembles the profile of Queen Victoria.

The river at Boscastle.

The harbour breakwaters and Profile Rock.

This view of Boscastle village has hardly changed at all from when this picture was taken in 1894. The castellated building is now the Wellington Hotel and the old mill wheel still turns, although not for its original purpose. The Wellington at Boscastle is one of the oldest coaching inns on the North Cornish coast. Boscastle, in fact, relied on horsedrawn coaches until as recently as the early 1920s. Indeed some old Boscastle folk can still recall the clatter of hooves and the clink of harness as the coaches rumbled down the Old Hill, all of which made the Wellington one of the very last posting houses in Britain.

An advertisement in *The Plymouth, Devonport and Stonehouse Herald*, dated 29 July 1849, reads: 'The Albion Omnibus, with first-rate horses and driver, leaves Saltash every Wednesday at ten o'clock precisely, passes Callington, and reaches Five Lanes twenty-past three, where it remains for one hour, and finally reaches Boscastle with Mail Coach regularity at seven o'clock. Fares, whole distance, 4s 6d inside, 3s 4d outside.'

There is alas no evidence that the Duke of Wellington 'with his hooked nose and piercing eye' stayed at the hotel, but sometime a Royal party stayed here which, it is believed, included Edward VII and a lady friend.

Coach and four outside the Wellington Hotel at Boscastle in 1913. The stage coaches first made their appearance in Cornwall at the beginning of the nineteenth century, the first mail coach route being from Exeter to Falmouth, via Launceston and Bodmin. The stages were always well-known and popular inns, such as the Wellington at Boscastle. Horses were changed at each stage. Half fare was charged passengers riding outside: those who paid for the luxury of a seat inside the coach were squeezed in like sardines in a tin in order to accommodate as many of the higher fare paying passengers as possible.

THE STREET, BOSCASTLE.

Valentines Serie

VILLAGE STREET, BOSCASTLE.

Three street scenes of Boscastle.

BOSCASTLE, FORE STREET   65312

Above: The Valency Valley is one of the loveliest valleys in the whole region, and largely unchanged from more than a hundred years ago when Thomas Hardy, the poet and novelist, walked along it with his fiancée, Emma Gifford, sister-in-law of the Vicar of St Juliot, a parish which stands high on its northern shoulder.

Left: Boscastle has two churches: this one, Forrabury, is set high on the cliffs; the other, at Minster, is hidden in a deep valley. The Norman church at Forrabury was largely refashioned in the nineteenth century. The doorway is fourteenth century.

The ladies of Boscastle came to their doors to pose for this
picture to be taken in the early 1900s. This was the
'affluent' part of the village in those days.

The road climbs up the valley
from Boscastle towards Tintagel.

At the well at Boscastle.

The cliffs of North Cornwall tower above Crackington Haven. It is now a very popular cove. Sometimes washed up on the beach here are the Cornish 'Little Trees', a deep water coral which branches like a miniature tree and has special powers according to an old legend. It is said that your house will never burn down if you keep a 'Little Tree' in it.

The Bude Canal was one of the most remarkable engineering feats of the nineteenth century. Work commenced on it in 1819, the idea being primarily to use the waterway for transporting sea sand, rich in minerals, from Bude to fertilise the land. A sea lock (*below*) was built, also a breakwater, at the Bude end. From there to Hele Bridge, Marhamchurch, the canal was a barge canal taking fifty foot long barges. After Hele Bridge, the canal became much narrower and was worked by tub boats. A series of remarkable incline planes made the canal almost an amphibious railway, the tub boats being fitted with wheels which enabled them to be hauled on rails up and down the planes. The canal, which finally closed in 1891, carried a great deal of merchandise in addition to sand, including culm – a type of 'steam' coal much used in steam traction engines – and coal brought to Bude from South Wales.

Above: Bude from the breakwater.

Below: Looking out to the breakwater in 1905 from the canal lock gate.

Waiting upon the tide in 1900.

Above: Bude was always a popular bathing resort. All the
bathing huts have now gone and there is a fine modern
swimming pool for those who do not want to venture into
the open sea. The tide goes out a long way and the golden
sands are extensive. Few people bask on the dunes today
as well wrapped up against the elements as the
Edwardian ladies shown in this picture.

Left: Our photographers pose on Bude breakwater in
1913.

Below and Right: Nanny Moore's Bridge at Bude was named after the nineteenth-century 'dipper' who lived in a nearby cottage. The old mill cottage, seen in this photograph, still stands but is now part of a bakery. Built into the wall of the cottage is a granite block carved with the initials 'AJA' and date 1589, as well as arms of the Dennis family. The initials stand for Anne and John Arundel. Lady Arundel built the tide mill known as Efford Mill in the sixteenth century and it was one of only five such mills recorded on the North Cornish coast.

Standing at this vantage point today the Strand at Bude looks much the same as in this picture.

Two views of The Strand and river at Bude. A quiet stroll
towards the cliffs was one of the attractions of the resort in
Edwardian days. Now this quiet path leads to a huge
carpark.

Bel Vue, looking Down, Bude

FALCON

HOTEL

Changing modes of transport at Bude. Left: Carriages and carts in Belle Vue, one of Bude's main shopping streets. *Below left:* Coach and Four outside the Falcon Hotel. *Below:* Early cars collecting passengers at the Falcon.

Breakwater at Bude 1905. The sea at Bude is reputed to be
heard ten miles away.

An attractive old town, Stratton has retained much of its
picturesque charm. In days gone by its inhabitants were
renowned for being independent and fearless and at one
time its main industry was the tanning of leather. The
famous Reverend Robert Stephen Hawker of
Morwenstow lived at Stratton when his father was vicar
of the church seen in the background of this picture.

Stratton no longer looks like it does in this photograph
but it still has narrow drangways leading to little hidden
squares around which cluster pretty houses and cottages.

West Street, Kilkhampton.

The A39 trunk road runs through Kilkhampton and the
quiet street shown in this photograph is now part of it.
On the left is the church, in front of which stands the war
memorial. Kilkhampton stands 600 feet above sea level
and its tall church tower can be seen for many miles
around. The church's fine Norman doorway is famous
and the church has a notable collection of bench ends. The
famous Grenville family lived in Kilkhampton and several
of them are buried in the magnificent church, where there
is a Grenville chapel.

Marhamchurch is a spacious village and was at one time an important 'junction' on the Bude Canal for here was the first of the incline planes and the big barges from Bude discharged their cargoes into smaller tub boats for transmission inland. The church tower at Marhamchurch has long been a landmark for mariners in the Bristol Channel.

Week St Mary.

Published by Senior Brothers, Holsworthy.

Thomasine Bonaventure is the name always associated with Week St Mary. She was a humble shepherd girl who was taken off to London in the sixteenth century by a rich merchant and subsequently became the wife of three lords in turn, the last being Sir John Percival, a Lord Mayor of London. She was a great benefactress and among her good work was endowing a chantry in the church. The church is seen in the background in this picture and on the right is the Methodist chapel.

S. Stephens.

The ancient town which climbs up the hill to the castle.
That was one writer's description of Launceston. The
keep of the Norman castle dominates the town. This view
is taken from the parish of St Stephens and an old rhyme
says 'St Stephens was a market town when Launceston
was a fuzzy down'.

The Southgate (*right*) was one of the gatehouses in the
town walls of Launceston. Outside there used to be a
moat and drawbridge. From the sixteenth century
onwards it was a prison until in 1884 the rooms were
converted into a museum. Now it houses an art gallery. A
prominent feature which was removed a few years ago
was the sycamore tree which grew out of the masonry and
can be seen in this picture.

Old Hill in Launceston is very steep but was one time the main road from the town to Newport and roads leading north. As a coaching road it must have been very dangerous. It still retains much of its old character and many of the houses are unchanged in appearance from when this picture was taken.

Right: Newport Square at Launceston was at one time an important part of the town for from a granite pillar in the old roundhouse on the left Launceston's Members of Parliament were elected.

This part of Launceston was all swept away in a town
improvement scheme after World War II. It was one of the
most picturesque areas of the town although many of the
dwellings were without modern amenities.

Prockter's Ironmongery and Cycle shop was one of the
long standing businesses in Launceston and it later
became Prockter & Kent before closure some years ago.
'Iron' was the operative word in the ironmongery side of
the business because the firm stocked a huge range of
farm and garden tools as well as iron saucepans, kettles
etc.

With all the hills around Launceston a bicycle hardly seems the ideal form of transport but in 1899 Messrs Prockter held a Cycle Show in the Western Rooms, Launceston, the premises now occupied by the *Cornish & Devon Post* newspaper. There must have been a demand and doubtless the 'young bloods' of the town found a bicycle a much more sophisticated form of transport than a horse!

Launceston was en fete, albeit in a subdued way as befitted the solemn occasion, when the Prince of Wales (later King Edward VIII) laid the foundation stone of the war memorial in the Square in 1920. The war memorial was erected on the site of the Butter Market which had, in its turn, succeeded the Assize Hall which formerly stood on the site. The quarter jacks, carved from oak in 1642, which had adorned the Assize Hall were later to find a permanent home below the clock on the front of the Town Hall, where they still strike the quarter hours. The clock was also moved from the Butter Market.

When the Butter Market was removed from Launceston Square in 1920 in order that a war memorial be erected in its place there was something of an outcry in the town, although it was muted because of the very nature of the structure which was to take its place. However, there was no sign of discord when the war memorial was unveiled on Sunday, 30 October 1921 by Mr J.C. Williams, Lord Lieutenant of Cornwall, in the presence of the Mayor of Launceston, Councillor James Treleaven, and a large crowd of townspeople.

During World War I Launceston Town Hall was turned into a military hospital and was staffed by local doctors and Red Cross nurses. Mr Arthur Venning of Launceston has recorded a story that the matron ensured that the convalescent patients would not 'go out on the town' at night by confiscating their trousers! A number of the voluntary helpers at the military hospital later formed the Launceston St John Ambulance Brigade.

The façade of J.S. Eyre & Co.'s Mineral Water Manufactory still exists in Castle Dyke, Launceston. Its distinctive decoration is the grouping of three Hamilton type bottles at the very top. These bottles with their pointed ends and stamped with the firm's name are now very much collectors' items and occasionally appear in antique shops in the town. The actual manufactory closed down some years ago and the premises have since been used for a variety of purposes.

Everyone today thinks of that popular Cornish newspaper the *Cornish and Devon Post* as having its premises at Western Buildings, Launceston, but it has not always been there. When it was just the *Launceston Weekly News* it was published from much smaller premises opposite St Mary's Church, premises which later became a photographer's shop and studio, then a hairdresser's establishment and is now a shop selling guns and other sporting equipment. In this photograph the building was decorated for some special occasion, possibly a royal visit.

'Keep for the album' wrote the sender of this postcard to someone in Lancashire. The village is in the parish of Morwenstow.

Hawker – the Reverend Robert Stephen Hawker, Vicar of Morwenstow for forty-one years, was well-known as a poet and writer and he built himself a little hut on the cliffs overlooking the Atlantic, where he could sit in solitude and write or just meditate. The hut was built from driftwood which Hawker brought up from the shore beneath the cliffs and it is now the National Trust's smallest property.

Sadly a fire in November 1968 destroyed the thatched roof of the Bush Inn at Morwenstow and it was replaced by a slate one. It is one of the oldest buildings in the village and has a genuine haunted reputation.

Not all postcards were views – some were amusing.
Nearly every seaside town and village had its own
holiday card such as these at one time.

On the Look Out

At TREBARWITH.

"This is our denner."

Father like mate and tatie best
Mother like turmut and mate
Boy Jack want all mate
Boy Tom like lickey best
an' the maidens edden pertic'lar 'tall.

The Cornish pasty is made nowhere else in the world like it is in Cornwall. Translation: Mate and tatie = meat and potatoes; turmut and mate = turnip and meat; all mate = all meat; lickey = leeks.

A Bright and ✛
Happy BIRTHDAY.

Greetings true and tender,
Affection loyal and ...
...strong, Best Wishes ...
From the sender,
Is what this ...
...brings along.

SYD.

Some cards contained birthday wishes.

It's miles better here than
at school.

At Trebarwith.

MILES

A HAPPY BIRTHDAY ~
LITTLE GIRL

To a sweet little, neat little
girl I know
Who thinks she is getting
quite old,
But the older she grows she is more
like a rose
Whose petals in sweetness unfold

Tonacombe is one of the great houses of farthest North
Cornwall. The approach is quaintly called Street. Hidden
from the road is one of the outstanding examples of a
fifteenth-century manor in the Westcountry. S.P.B. Mais
thought it 'worth crossing a continent to see', and one
interesting literary theory is that Charles Kingsley used
Tonacombe as the setting for the chapel in *Westward Ho!*
Dating from the reign of the first Elizabeth, it has three
courtyards and a walled garden. Inside, the hall is open to
the roof. There is a minstrel's gallery and a priest's hiding
place. Moreover it has a genuinely haunted reputation
and there is a belief that Katherine Kempthorne, who was
buried in Morwenstow Church in 1613, makes ghostly
appearances at Tonacombe.

An interior view of the hall at Tonacombe taken by
Herbert Hughes in the early 1900s.

Tonacombe is still lived in by a member of the family who has owned it for many years.

The boundary of Cornwall and Devon is no bad place at which to end a tour of North Cornwall – either in the old days or today – this is essentially border territory. It is Hawker country, for the spirit of individuality and eccentricity of that famous clerical character lives on. Here on these cliffs of North Cornwall, you can get a sense of perspective. Here time and Man have made little impact.

Also Available

GATEWAY TO CORNWALL
by Joan Rendell, 72 photographs.
Joan Rendell writes about Launceston and District — a highly personal portrait of the place, some of its past and people. 'I have attempted to make this book different from other publications about the area…'
'A delight to lovers of the local scene and its historic background.'
Arthur Venning, The Editor, Cornish & Devon Post

HAWKER COUNTRY
by Joan Rendell. 40 photographs, letters and map.
Hawker Country is an area of North Cornwall, embracing some cruel, dramatic coastline and beautiful countryside: a corner of the Westcountry immortalised by the great Parson Hawker of Morwenstow.
'A book about that Prince of clerical eccentrics and the places associated with him … contains many pictures of great interest.'
The Church Times

ALONG THE BUDE CANAL
by Joan Rendell, 49 photographs and map.
The Bude Canal is — or was — a vanishing piece of Cornish history. However, now, thanks to the brilliant researching of Joan Rendell and her ability to get Cornish folk — related to the Canal — to talk, she resurrects it all. Through her words and pictures, we see it flowing and working once again.
'…the book makes a valuable contribution to the history of the Bude Canal. Its easily readable style and modest price should ensure a ready sale to both canal enthusiast and holidaymaker alike. I recommend it to all readers of Waterways World.'
Kenneth R. Clew

CORNISH CHURCHES
by Joan Rendell. 60 photographs and drawings.
Here in her fifth title for Bossiney Joan Rendell explores many of Cornwall's lovely churches. Music and myths, art and architecture, personalities past and present are only some of the facets of her journey across the Cornish landscape.
'…an author who is well qualified to take us on a tour of Cornish Churches…extremely readable.'
Cornish Guardian

THE CRUEL CORNISH SEA
by David Mudd. 65 photographs.
David Mudd selects more than 30 Cornish shipwrecks, spanning 400 years, in his fascinating account of seas at a coastline that each year claim their toll of human lives.
'This is an important book.'
Lord St Levan, the Cornish Times.

CASTLES OF CORNWALL
by Mary and Hal Price. 78 photographs and map.
St Catherine's Castle and Castle Dore both at Fowey, Restormel near Lostwithiel, St Mawes, Pendennis at Falmouth, St Michael's Mount, Tintagel, Launceston and Trematon near Saltash. Mary and Hal Price on this tour of Cornwall explore these nine castles.
'…a lavishly illustrated narrative that is both historically sound and written in a compelling and vivid style that carries the reader along from one drama to the next.'
Pamela Leeds, The Western Evening Herald

VIEWS OF OLD CORNWALL
by Sarah Foot.
Nearly 200 old picture postcards from the Peter Dryden collection, with text by Sarah Foot, all combine to recall Cornwall as she once was.
'…will be certain to start the talk flowing of days gone by.'
The Cornishman

THE CORNISH YEAR BOOK
Over 150 photographs and drawings.
Writers, artists and photographers have all combined to reveal facets of Cornwall and a Cornish way of life through spring, summer, autumn and winter.

A CORNISH CAMERA
by George Ellis and Sarah Foot.
More than 200 photographs taken by George Ellis, the doyen of Cornish press photographers. Cornwall at work and play in war and peace; town and countryside and coast; personalities and customs; triumphs and tragedies. Sarah Foot's text adds the stories behind these pictures.
'A delightfully nostalgic look back at the last 40 years in the County.'
Sunday Independent

AROUND LAND'S END

Michael Williams explores the end and the beginning of Cornwall. Wrecks and legends, the Minack Theatre, Cable & Wireless, Penwith characters and customs, lighthouses and Lyonesse all feature. 90 photographs, many of them from Edwardian and Victorian times, help to tell the story.

THE CORNISH EDWARDIANS

by David Mudd. 66 illustrations.
Here in words and pictures is David Mudd's portrait of Cornwall in the Edwardian reign.
'Gives excellent "colour slide" flash backs to a time which helped make Cornwall what it is today.'
Phil Stoneham, Cornwall Courier

KING ARTHUR COUNTRY in CORNWALL THE SEARCH for the REAL ARTHUR

by Brenda Duxbury, Michael Williams and Colin Wilson.
Over 50 photographs and 3 maps.
An exciting exploration of the Arthurian sites in Cornwall and Scilly, including the related legends of Tristan and Iseult, with The Search for the Real Arthur by Colin Wilson.
'...provides a refreshing slant on an old story linking it with the present.'
Caroline Righton. The Packet Newspapers

CURIOSITIES OF CORNWALL

By Michael Williams. 62 photographs.
Eccentric architecture; customs—curious, Cornish and Royal; curious characters and a curiosity that grew into invention and innovation; the deep hole at Delabole; the question witch or saint? ... all these and much more prove that Cornwall has more than her share of curiosities.
'...a fascinating new book...avid collectors of offbeat gems of knowledge, whether they belong to the county or not, will welcome it as a treasure...'
Pamela Leeds, The Western Evening Herald

STRANGE HAPPENINGS IN CORNWALL

by Michael Williams. 35 photographs.
Strange shapes, and strange characters; healing and life after death; reincarnation and Spiritualism; murders and mysteries are only some of the contents in this fascinating book.
'...this eerie Cornish collection.'
David Foot, Western Daily Press

CORNISH MYSTERIES

by Michael Williams. 40 photographs.
Cornish Mysteries is a kind of jig-saw puzzle in words and pictures. The power of charming, mysterious shapes in the Cornish landscape, the baffling murder case of Mrs Hearn are just some fascinating ingredients.
'...superstitions, dreams, murder, Lyonesse, the legendary visit of the boy Jesus to Cornwall, and much else. Splendid, and sometimes eerie, chapters.'
The Methodist Recorder

SUPERNATURAL IN CORNWALL

by Michael Williams. 24 photographs.
'...a book of fact, not fiction ... covers not only apparitions and things that go bump in the night, but also witchcraft, clairvoyancy, spiritual healing, even wart charming...'
Jenny Myerscough on BBC
'Serious students of ghost-hunting will find a fund of locations.'
Graham Danton on Westward TV

SUPERSTITION AND FOLKLORE

by Michael Williams. 45 photographs.
Romany reflections, old country customs, interviews with superstitious people, folklore from both Devon and Cornwall, omens and coincidences are all featured.
'...has all the ingredients of a mini-bestseller.'
Cornwall Courier

VIEWS OF OLD DEVON

Rosemary Anne Lauder provides the text for more than 200 old postcards, evocative of a world and a way of life that has gone. Words and pictures combine to produce a book that will delight all who love Devon.
'Only the camera can turn back the clock like this.'
The Sunday Independent

VIEWS OF OLD PLYMOUTH

by Sarah Foot.
Words and old pictures combine to recall Plymouth as it once was: a reminder of those great times past and of the spirit of the people of Plymouth.
'This is a lovely nostalgia-ridden book and one which no real Plymothian will want to be without.'
James Mildren, The Western Morning News

LEGENDS OF CORNWALL

by Sally Jones. 60 photographs and drawings. Brilliantly illustrated with photographs and vivid drawings of legendary characters. A journey through the legendary sites of Cornwall, beginning at the Tamar and ending at Land's End.
'Highly readable and beautifully romantic…'
Desmond Lyons, Cornwall Courier

MY CORNWALL

A personal vision of Cornwall by eleven writers living and working in the county: Daphne du Maurier, Ronald Duncan, James Turner, Angela du Maurier, Jack Clemo, Denys Val Baker, Colin Wilson, C.C. Vyvyan, Arthur Caddick, Michael Williams and Derek Tangye, with reproductions of paintings by Margo Maeckelberghe and photographs by Bryan Russell.
'An ambitious collection of chapters.'
The Times, London

OCCULT IN THE WEST

by Michael Williams. Over 30 photographs. Michael Williams follows his successful **Supernatural in Cornwall** with further interviews and investigations into the Occult—this time incorporating Devon. Ghosts and clairvoyancy, dreams and psychic painting, healing and hypnosis are only some of the facets of a fascinating story.
'…provides the doubters with much food for thought.'
Jean Kenzie, Tavistock Gazette

THE CALL OF THE WEST

by Arthur Caddick
Selected lyric poems with a comic interlude.
'This book is as delightful as the reader can hope. The landscape, the seasons, the people, the history. Mr Caddick dips his lyric, his comic, his emotional pen—in turn—into the ink of life.
The Cornishman
'It's my belief that Arthur Caddick is the Dylan Thomas of Cornwall. Like Dylan Thomas he has the gift of touching our hearts.'
Derek Tangye

LEGENDS OF DEVON

by Sally Jones. 60 photographs and drawings. Devon is a mine of folklore and myth. Here in a journey through legendary Devon, Sally Jones brings into focus some fascinating tales, showing us that the line dividing fact and legend is an intriguing one.
'…Sally Jones has trodden the path of legendary Devon well…'
Tavistock Times

STRANGE STORIES FROM DEVON

by Rosemary Anne Lauder and Michael Williams. 46 photographs.
Strange shapes and places—strange characters—the man they couldn't hang, and a Salcombe mystery, the Lynmouth disaster and a mysterious house are only some of the strange stories.
'A riveting read'.
The Plymouth Times
'…well-written and carefully edited'
Monica Wyatt, Teignmouth Post & Gazette

CURIOSITIES OF DEVON

by Michael Williams.
Michael Williams explores strange and unusual aspects of a county of contrasts; curious customs and characters, strange architecture and landscapes, and highly individual Dartmoor characters. There are visits to the Finch Foundry at Sticklepath and Arlington Court.

MY DEVON

Ten writers writing about their Devon: Hugh Caradon, Judy Chard, Andrew Cooper, Robin Davidson, Daniel Farson, Sarah Foot, Clive Gunnell, James Mildren, Mary and Hal Price.
'…ten writers' impressions of their favourite places…the personal approach warms and enlivens…'
Herald Express

FOLLOWING THE TAMAR

by Sarah Foot. 63 photographs and map.
Sarah Foot is the Tamar's inevitable author, living only a mile from its banks, seeing it every day from her Cornish home, and truly loving it.
'…both a labour of love and a work of subtle selection, combining the intriguing byways of local history and geography with a profusion of well-chosen black and white plates.'
Dick Benson-Gyles, The Western Evening Herald

We shall be pleased to send you our catalogue giving full details of our growing list of titles for Devon and Cornwall and forthcoming publications.

If you have difficulty in obtaining our titles, write direct to Bossiney Books, Land's End, St Teath, Bodmin, Cornwall.